A DOZEN A DAY

Technical Exercises
FOR THE PIANO
to be done each day
BEFORE practicing

by

Edna-Mae Burnam

THE WILLIS MUSIC COMPANY

To my family

A DOZEN A DAY

Many people do exercises every morning before they go to work.

Likewise—we should all give our fingers exercises every day BEFORE we begin our practicing.

The purpose of this book is to help develop strong hands and flexible fingers.

Do not try to learn the entire first dozen exercises the first week you study this book! Just learn two or three exercises and do them each day *before* practicing. When these are mastered, add another, then another, and keep adding until the twelve can be played perfectly.

When the first dozen— or Group I— has been mastered and perfected, Group II may be introduced in the same manner.

When the entire book is finished, any of the groupings may be transposed to different keys. In fact, this should be encouraged.

EDNA MAE BURNAM

Group I
1. Walking and Running

1st time—legato (smooth, connected)
2nd time—staccato (sharp, detached)

3/17-24

col

1 a t a 2 a t a 3 a t a 4 a t a   1 a t a 2 a t a + 3 a + a 4 a t a   1 a t a 2 a t a

2. Skipping

3/31-4/7   col

legato—staccato

3. Hopping

col

staccato

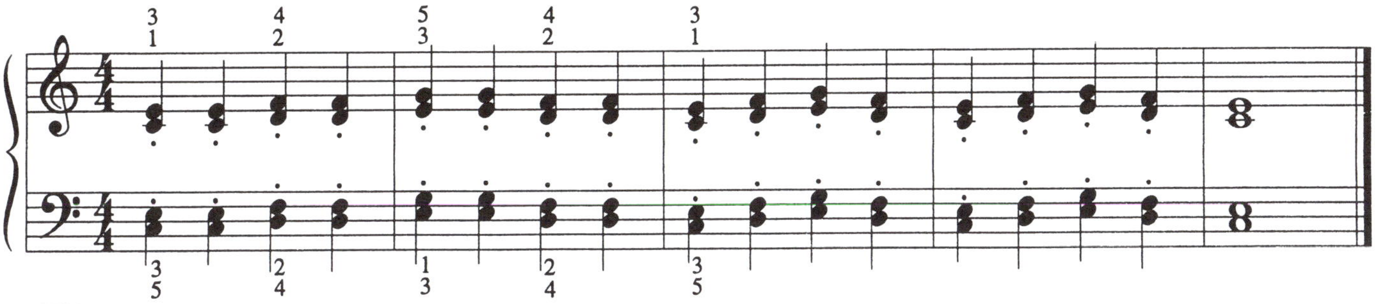

4. Deep Breathing

5/12-19

5. Deep Knee Bend

6/2-9-23   Col
Ledger Line Rule
if there are 3 ledger lines
below the staff they spell ACE
reading from bottom
to top   E —
         C —
         A —

6. Stretching

Col

L.H.

7. Stretching Right Leg Up

8. Stretching Left Leg

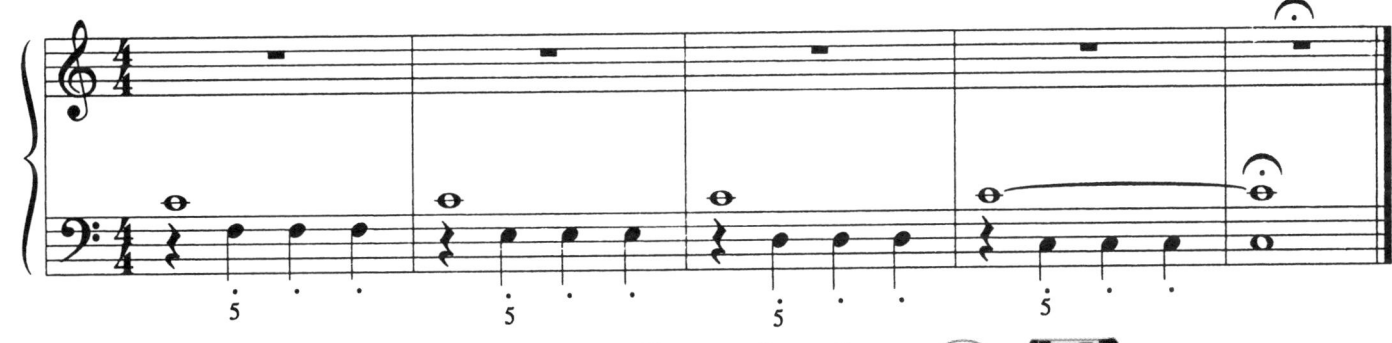

9. Cartwheels

10. The Splits

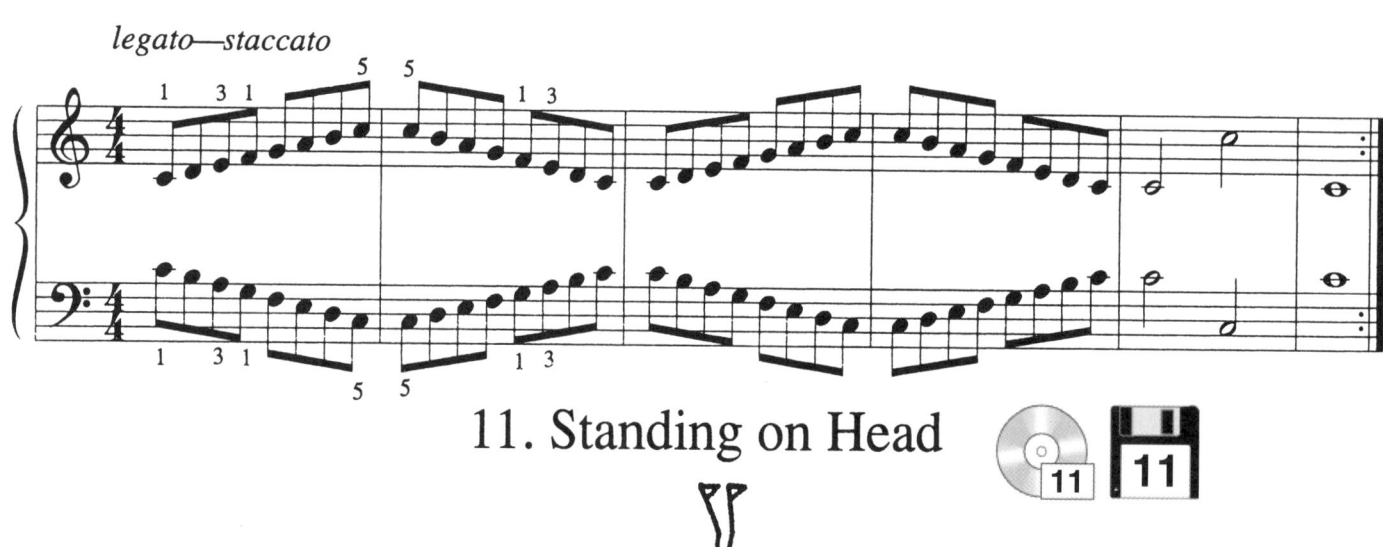

11. Standing on Head

12. Fit as a Fiddle and Ready To Go

Group II
1. Morning Stretch

2. Walking

legato—staccato

3. Running

legato—staccato

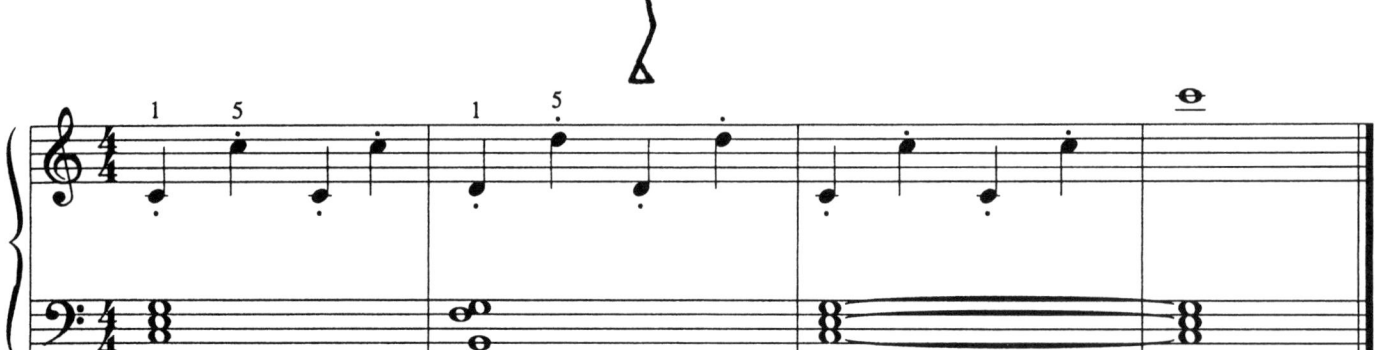

4. High Stepping

16 16

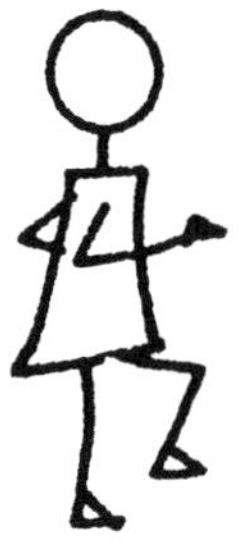

legato—staccato

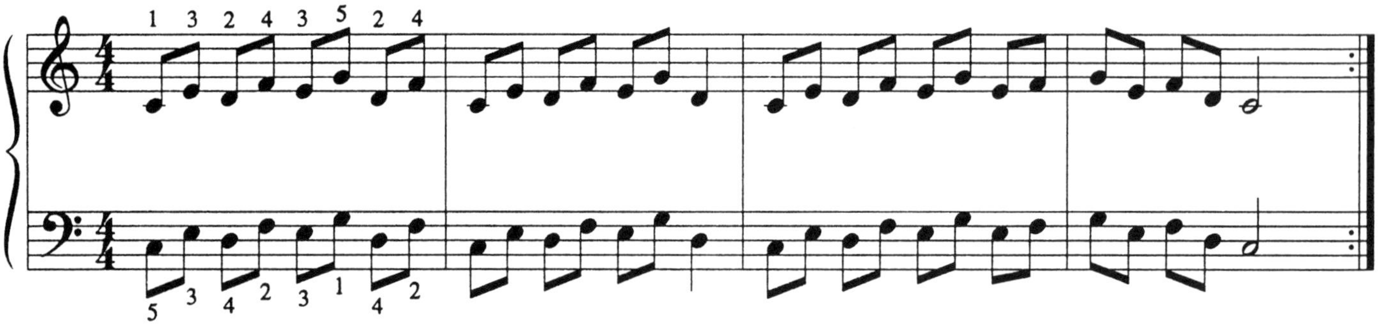

5. Jumping

17 17

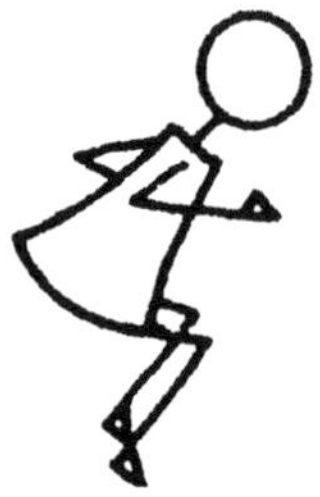

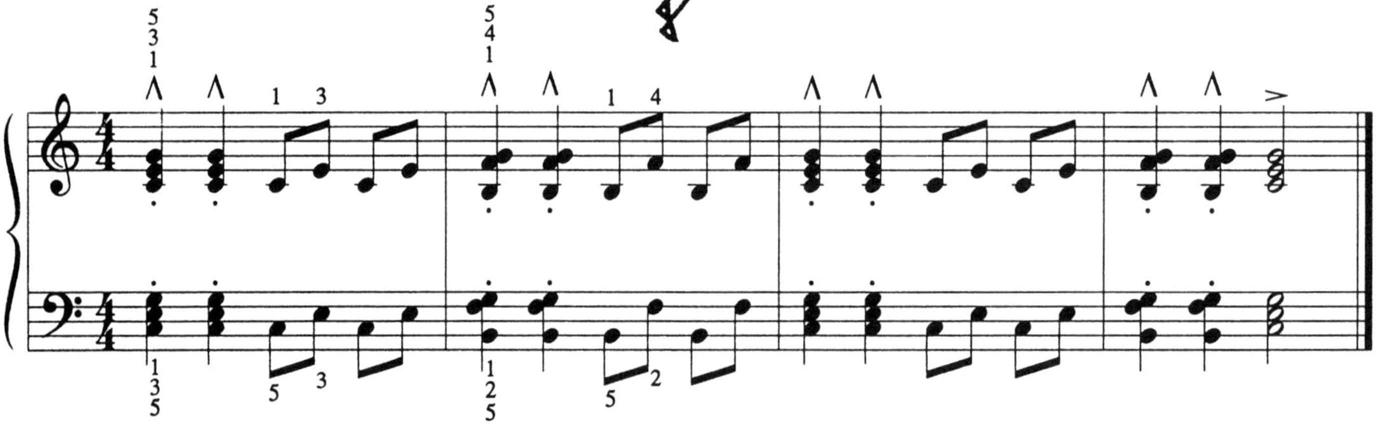

6. Kicking Right Leg

18 18

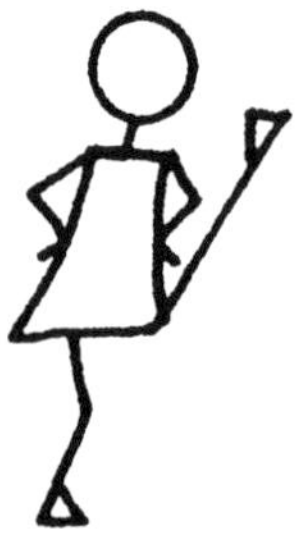

7. Kicking Left Leg

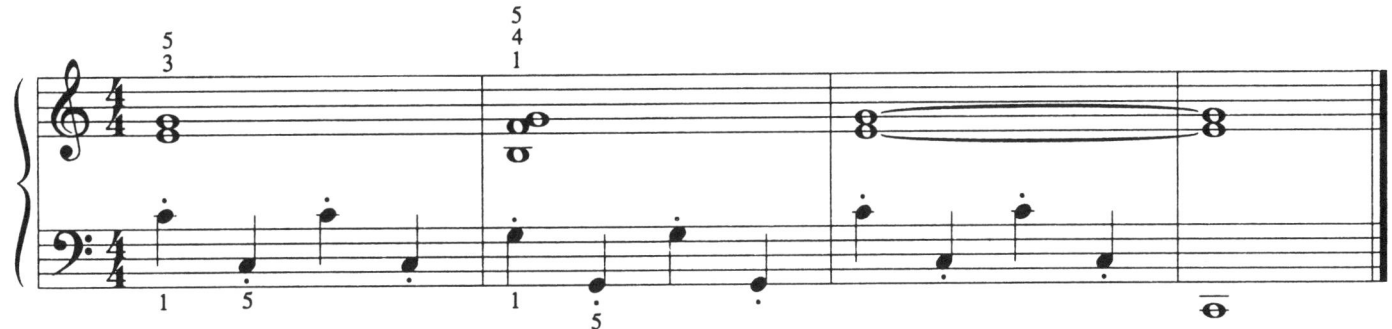

8. The Splits

9. Leg Work (lying down)

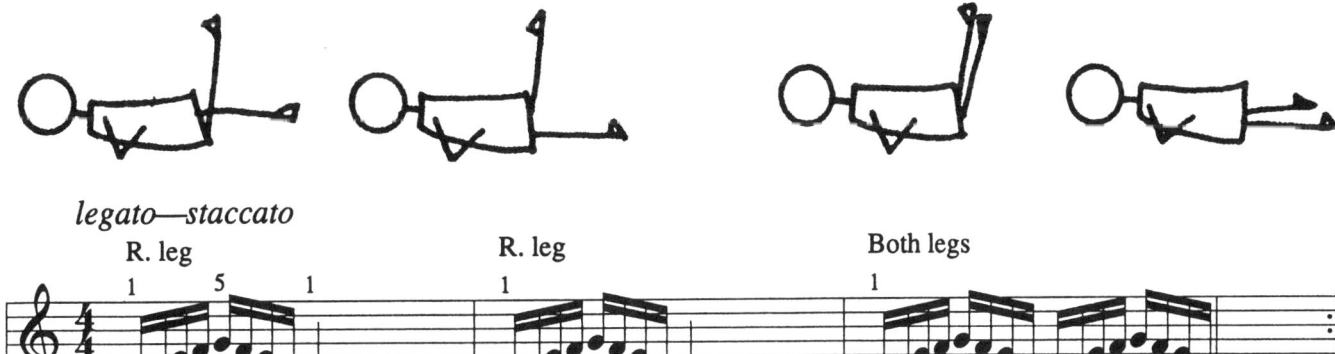

legato—staccato

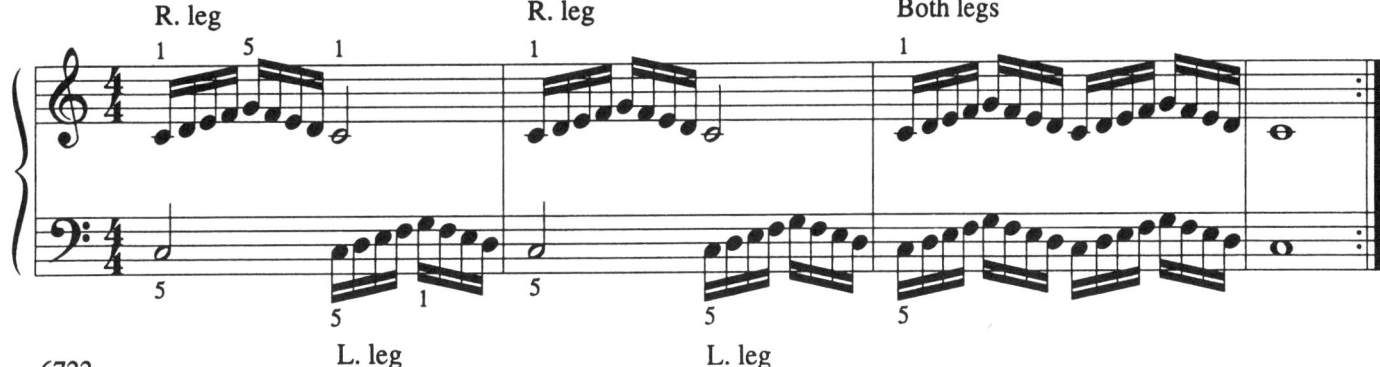

10. Sitting Up and Lying Down

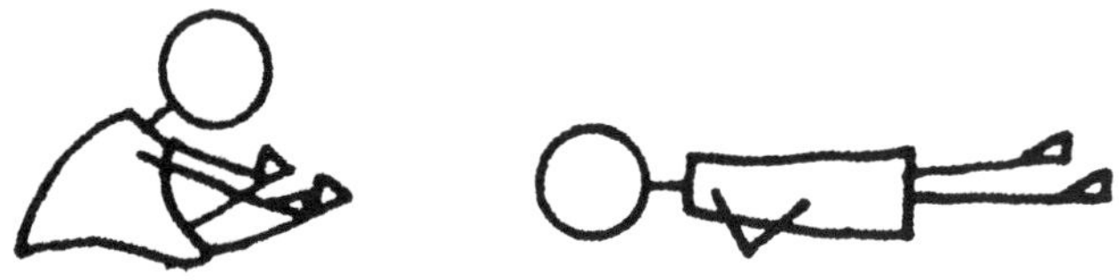

legato—staccato

11. A Hard Trick

Practice this first:

legato—staccato

Then practice this:

legato—staccato

Now do the whole trick:

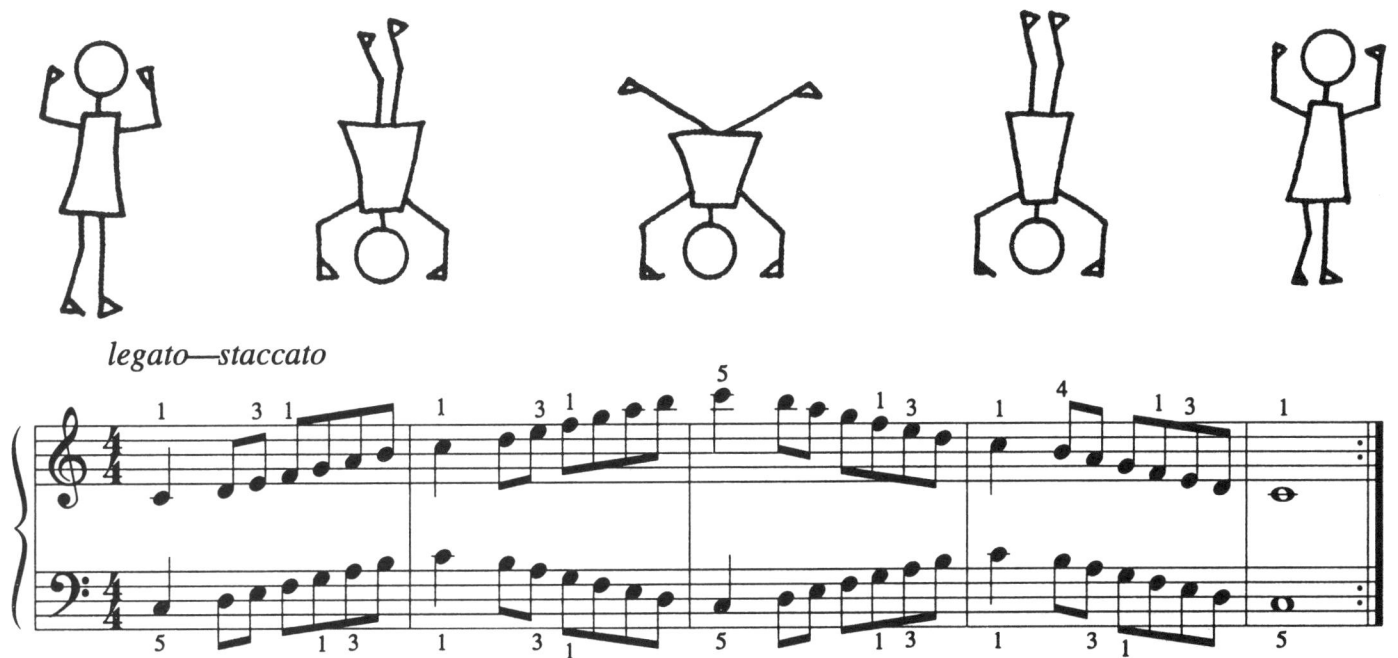

legato—staccato

12. Fit as a Fiddle and Ready To Go

Group III
4. Deep Breathing

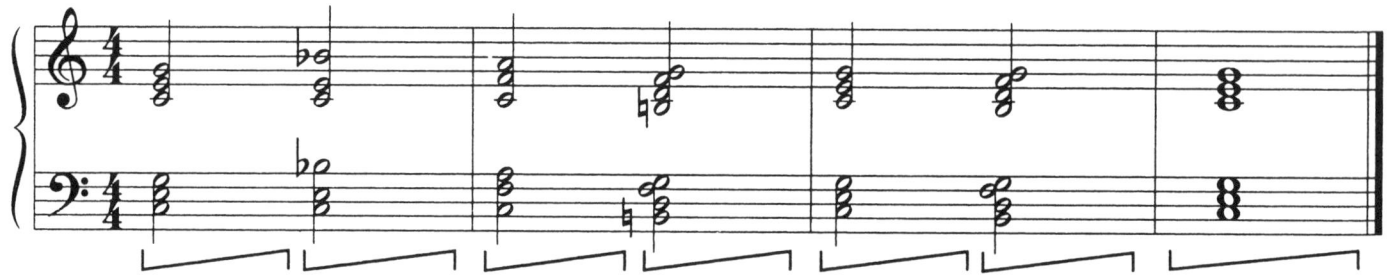

2. Rolling

legato—staccato

3. Climbing (in place)

legato—staccato

4. Tip-toe Running (in place)

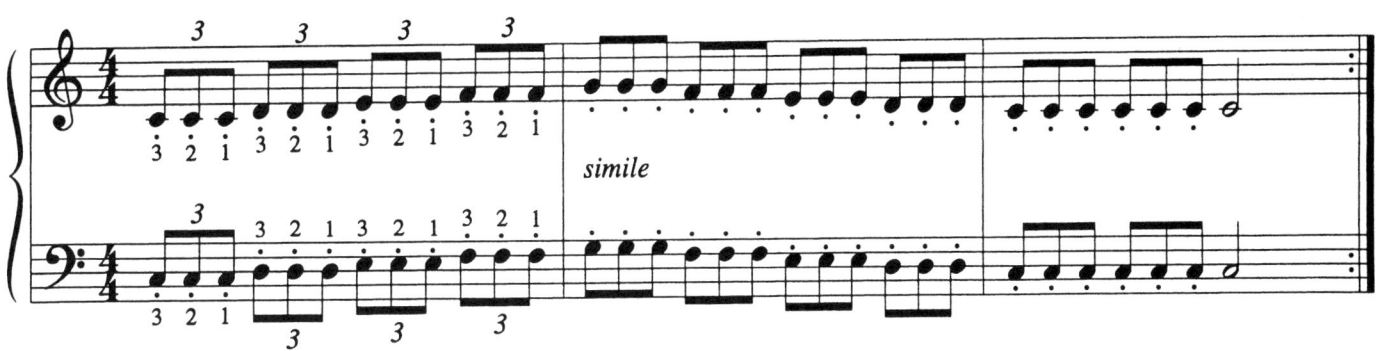

5. Baby Steps

legato—staccato

6. Giant Steps

7. Jumping Rope

8. Somersaults

9. Touching Toes

10. Ballet Exercise ("Entre chat quatre")

11. The Splits

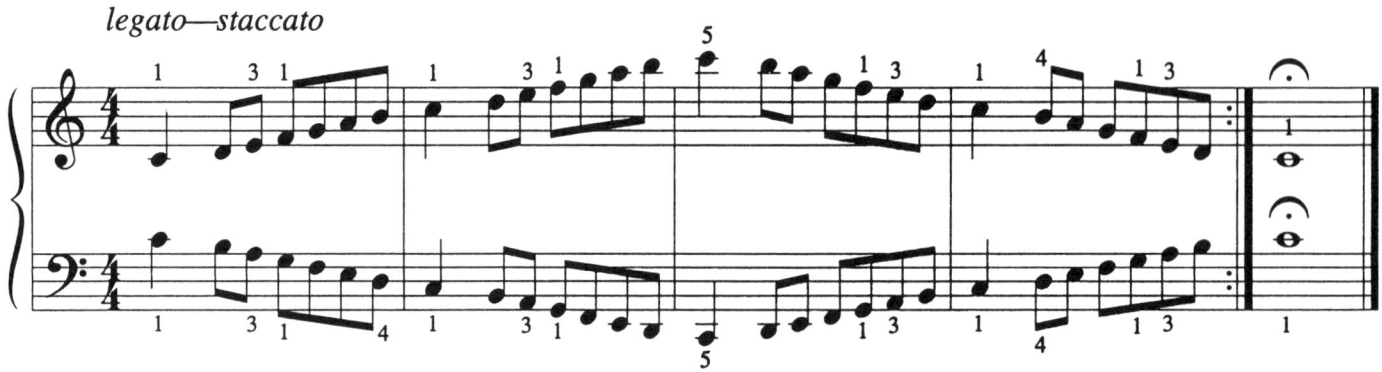

12. Fit as a Fiddle and Ready To Go

Group IV
1. Morning Stretch

2. Climbing (in place)

legato—staccato

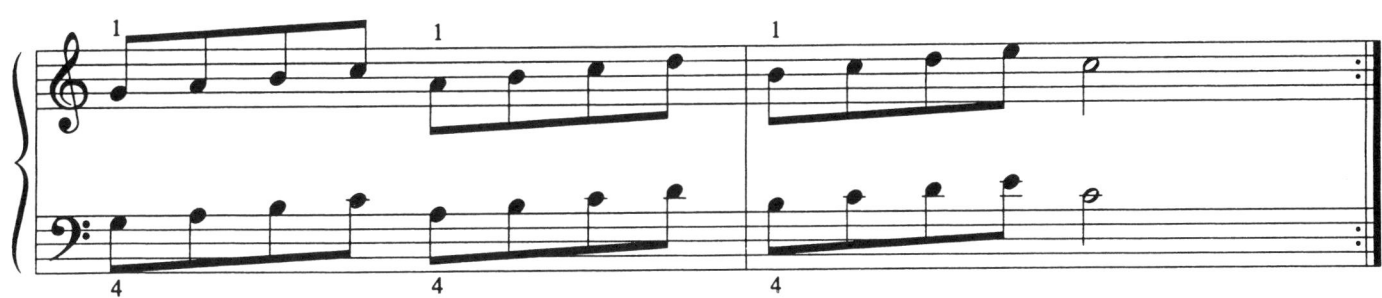

3. Tip-toe Running (in place)

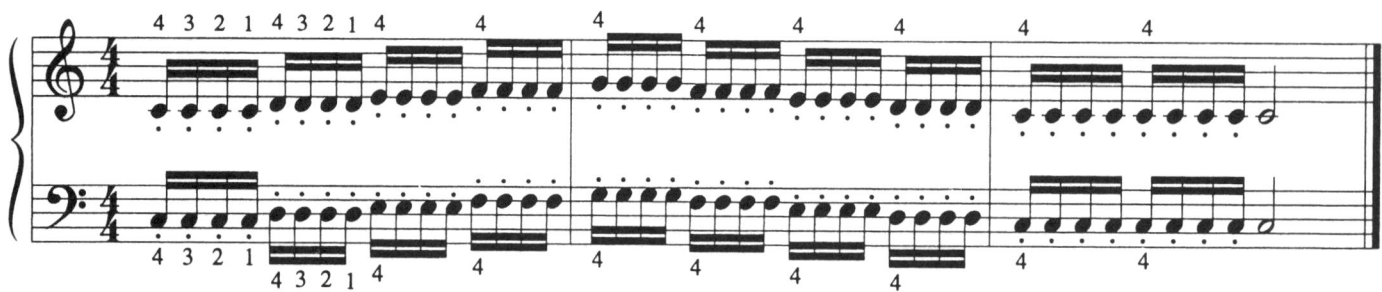

4. Running

legato—staccato

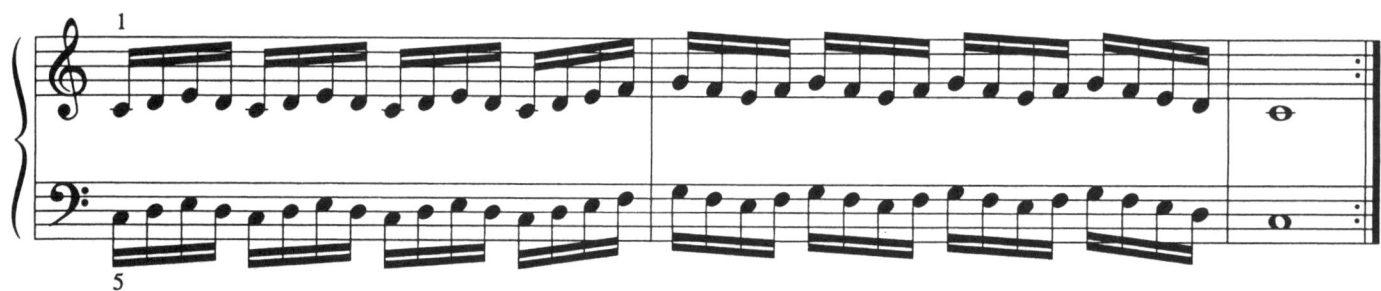

5. Cartwheels

6. Touching Toes

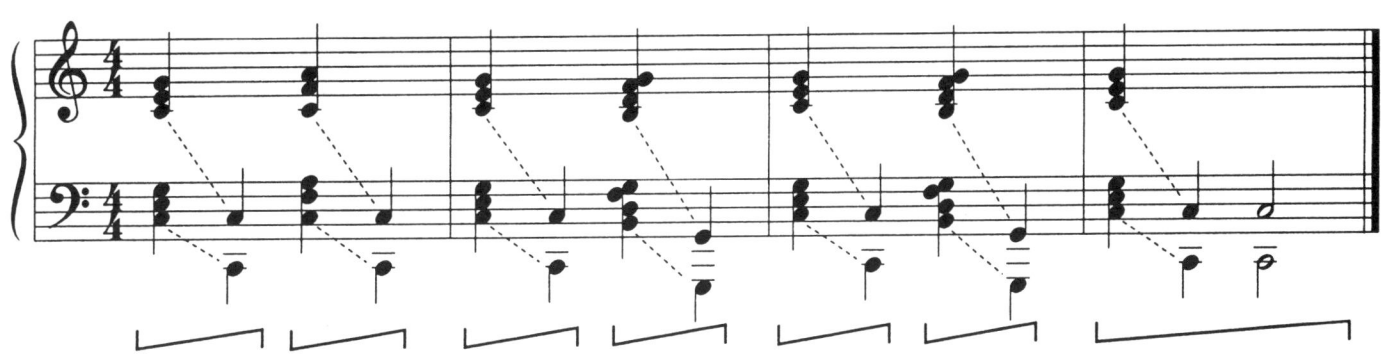

7. Hopping

8. Baby Steps

9. Giant Steps

10. Flinging Arms Out and Back

legato—staccato

11. Standing on Head

12. Fit as a Fiddle and Ready To Go

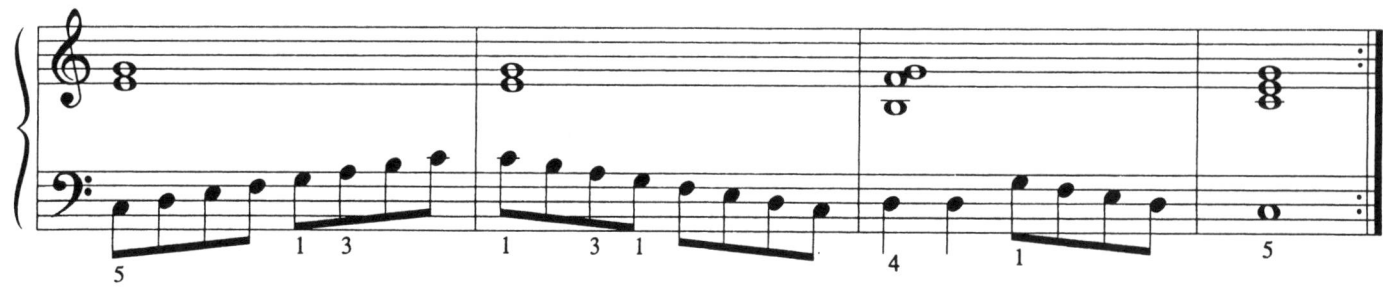

Group V
1. Deep Breathing

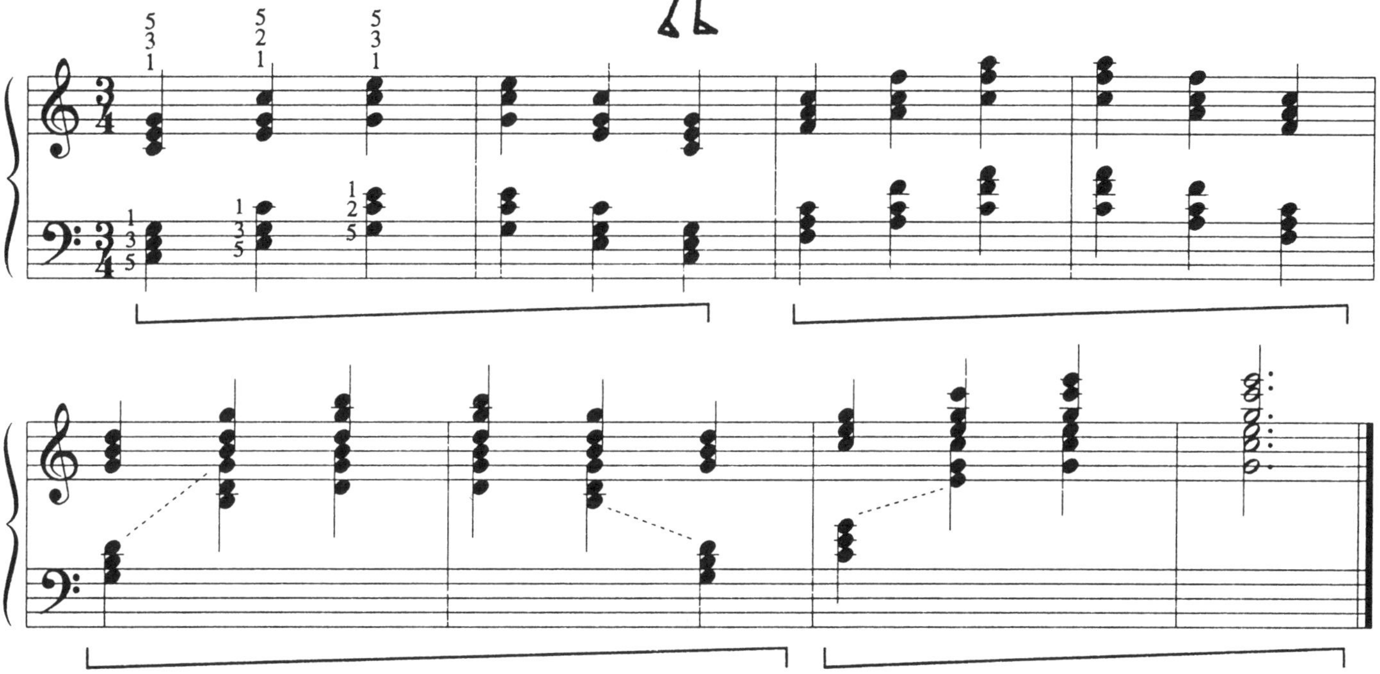

2. Touching Toes

3. Hopping

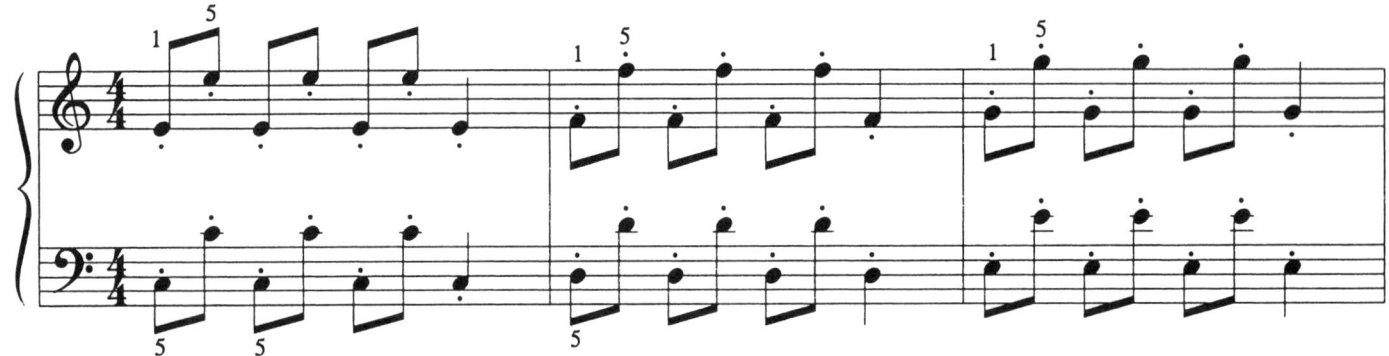

4. Climbing a Ladder

legato—staccato

5. Jumping Rope (Slow, and "Red Pepper")

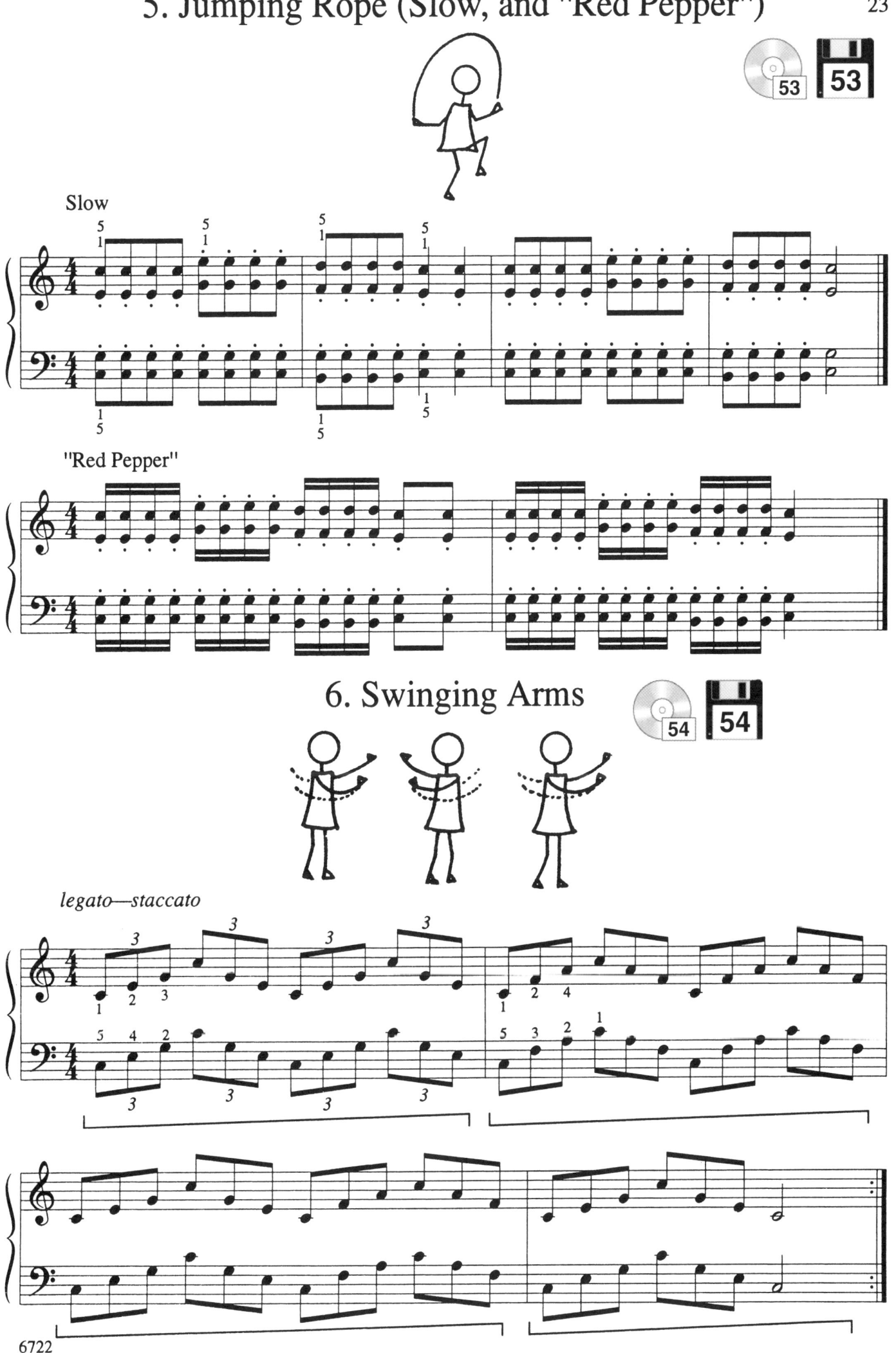

6. Swinging Arms

7. Hand Springs

8. Walking Like a Duck

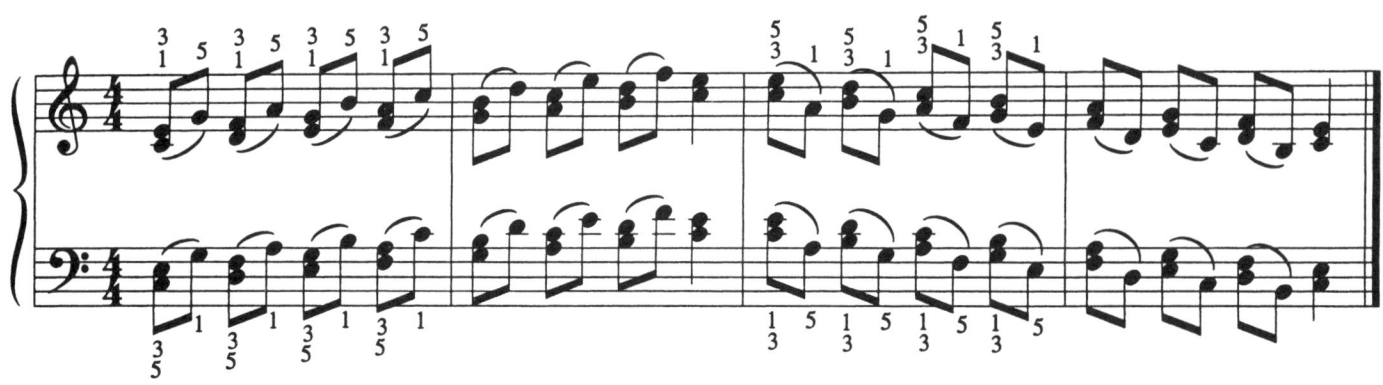

9. Bear Walk

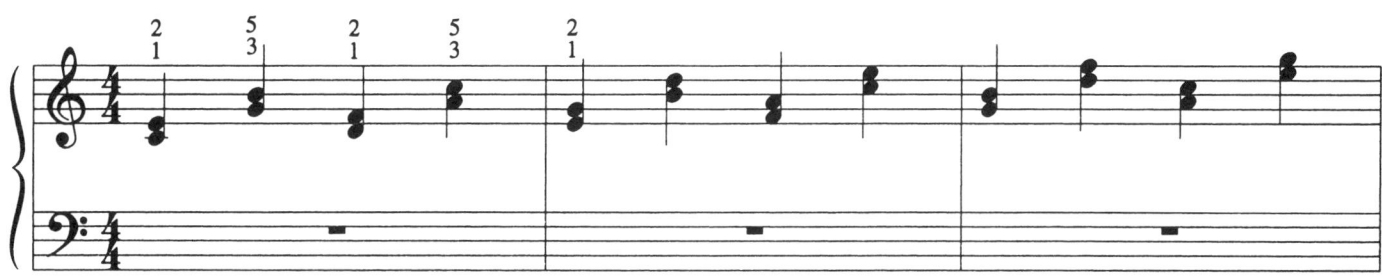

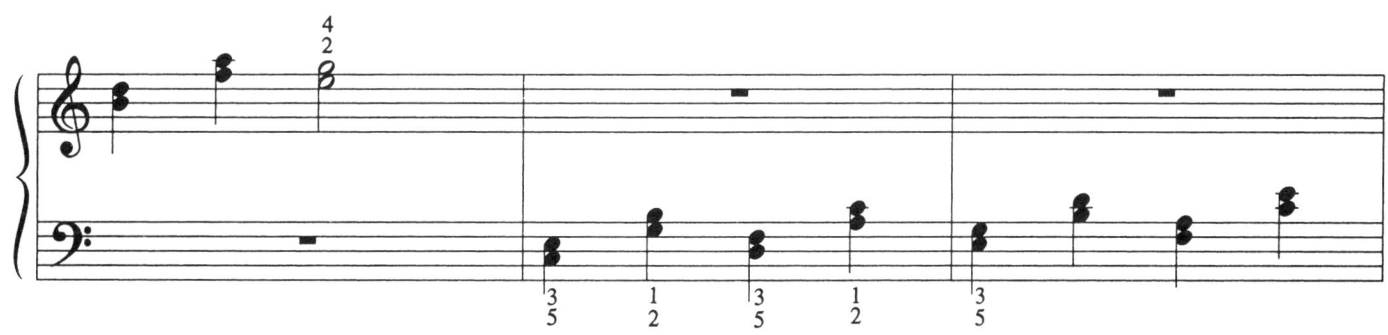

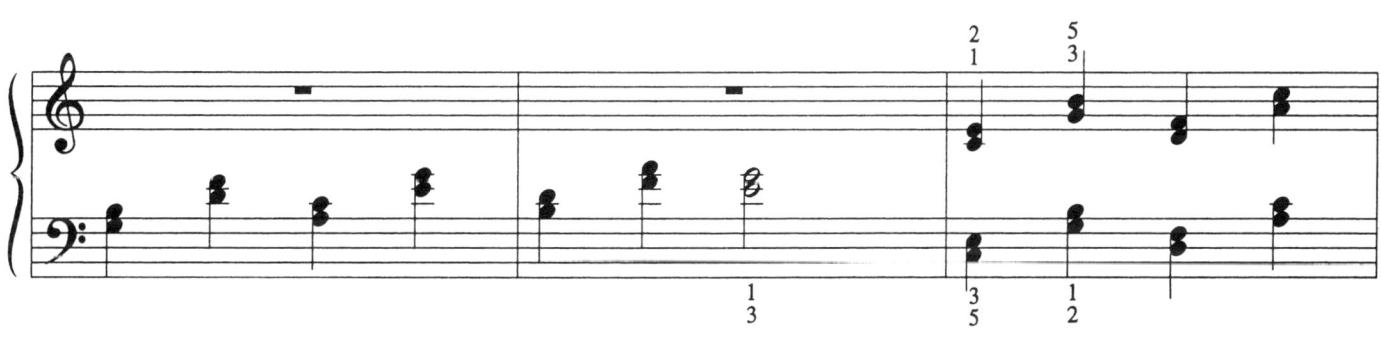

6722

10. Sliding Down the Bannister

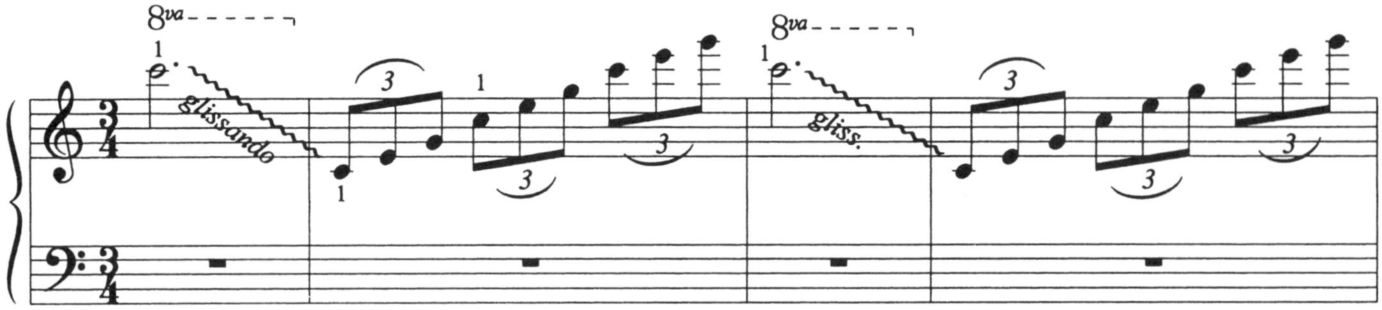

11. A Hard Trick

Practice this first:

legato—staccato

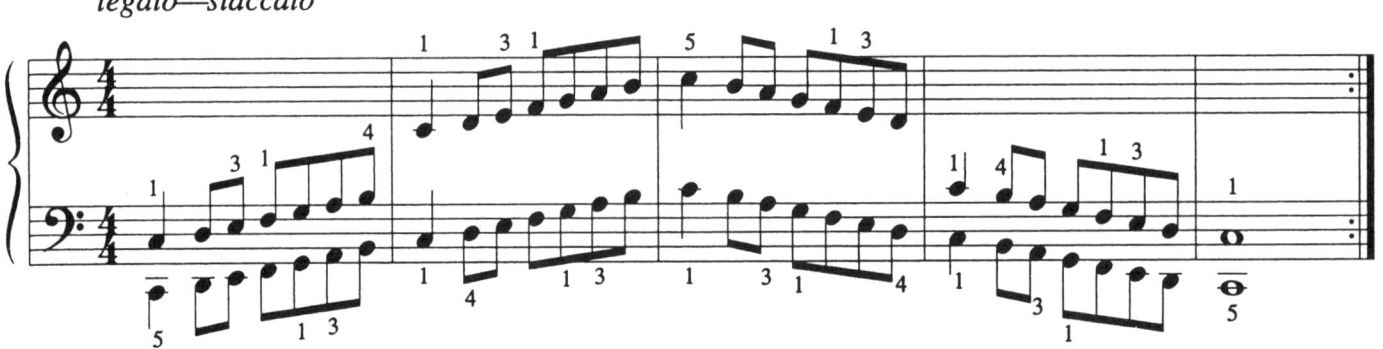

Now practice this:

legato—staccato

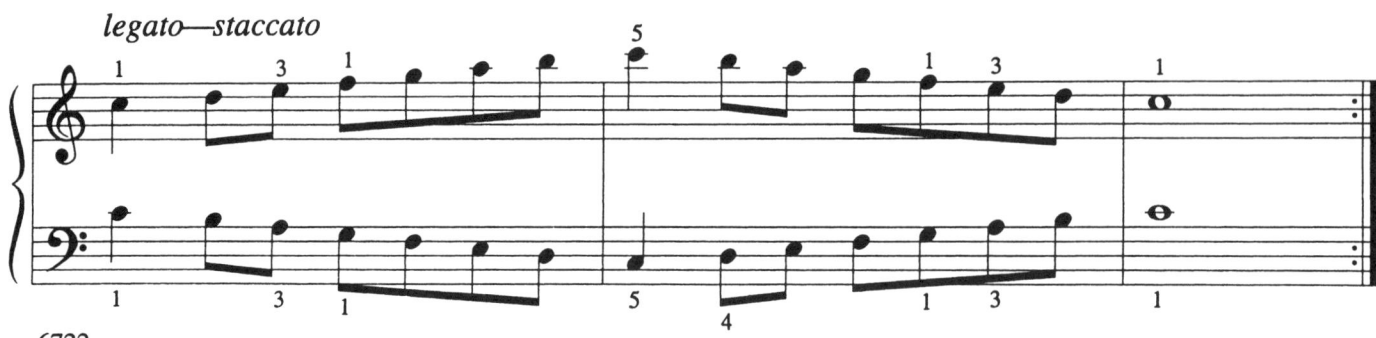

Now do the whole trick:

legato—staccato

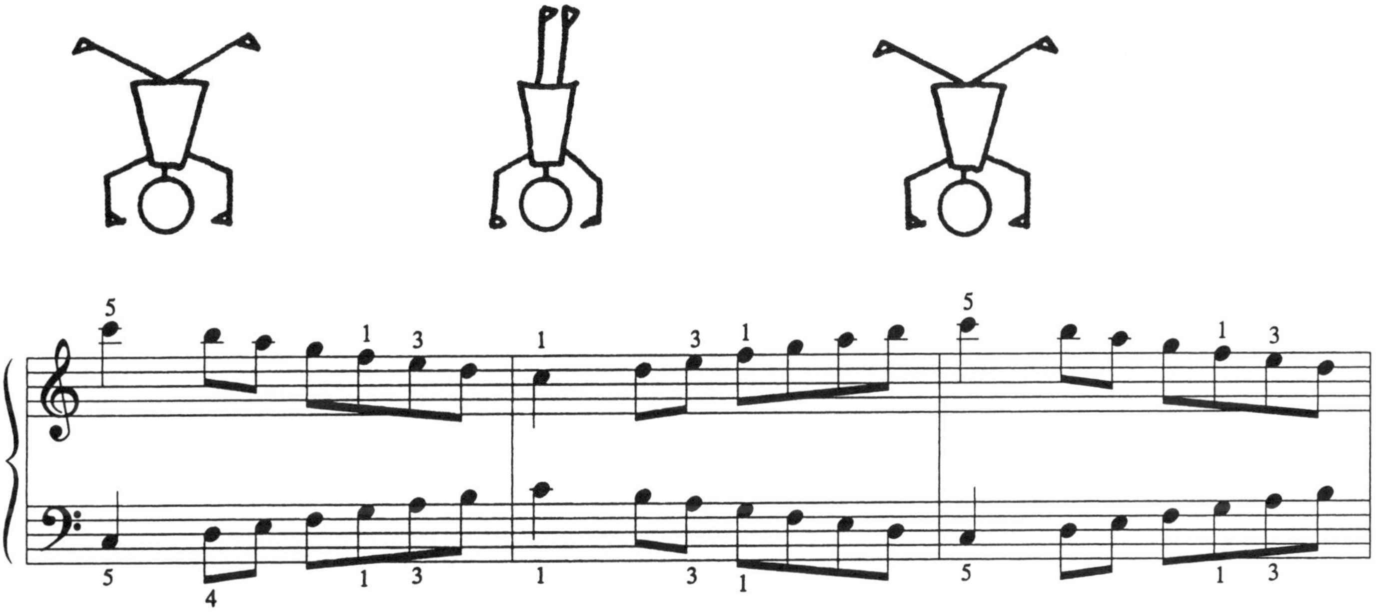

12. Fit as a Fiddle and Ready To Go

legato—staccato

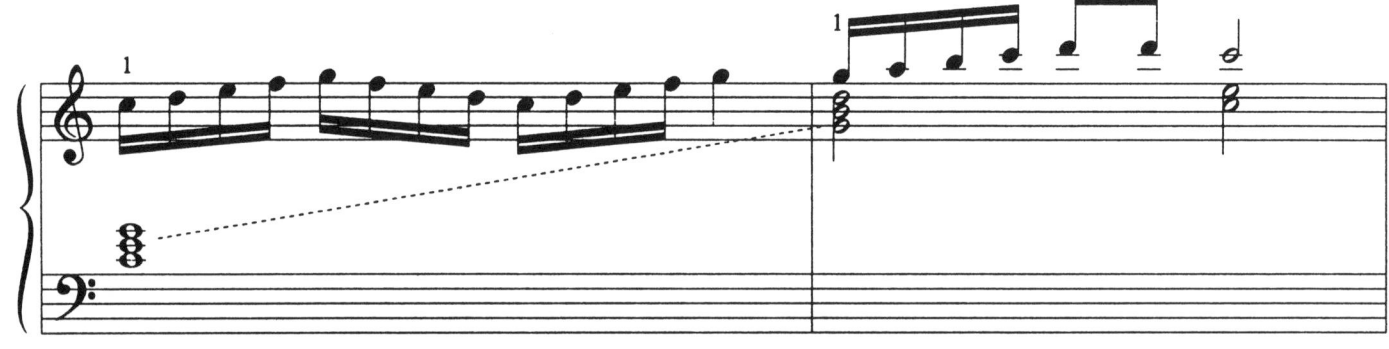